D0197375

My Date My Story

NO LONGER PROPERTY OF
ANYTHINK LIBRARIES/
RANGEVIEW LIBRARY DISTRICT

My Date My Story

True Stories of Modern Dating, Sex, and Heartbreak

JESSE STERN

Skyhorse Publishing

Copyright © 2018 by Jesse Stern

Chapter opener illustrations © Zlatina Gocheva

All rights reserved. No part of this book may be reproduced in any manner without the express written consent of the publisher, except in the case of brief excerpts in critical reviews or articles. All inquiries should be addressed to Skyhorse Publishing, 307 West 36th Street, 11th Floor, New York, NY 10018.

Skyhorse Publishing books may be purchased in bulk at special discounts for sales promotion, corporate gifts, fund-raising, or educational purposes. Special editions can also be created to specifications. For details, contact the Special Sales Department, Skyhorse Publishing, 307 West 36th Street, 11th Floor, New York, NY 10018 or info@skyhorsepublishing.com.

Skyhorse® and Skyhorse Publishing® are registered trademarks of Skyhorse Publishing, Inc.®, a Delaware corporation.

Visit our website at www.skyhorsepublishing.com.

10 9 8 7 6 5 4 3 2 1

Library of Congress Cataloging-in-Publication Data is available on file.

Cover design by Mona Lin

Print ISBN: 978-1-5107-3895-9
Ebook ISBN: 978-1-5107-3897-3

Printed in China

This is dedicated to you.

Those of you desperate for answers.

Those of you in pain.

Those of you who are healing.

Those of you who have made it to the other side,
where the agony is only a memory.

contents

x x x x x x x x x x x x x x x

introduction

The My Date My Story project started as a place for people to confess their first date stories.

It quickly became something very different.

Within a year, more than 100,000 people were discussing meaningful relationship issues, and were helping one another get through the modern complexities of dating.

People were not only finding support and understanding, but also a human connection.

The stories that pour in each day cover every facet of modern day relationships—many are from people who have been deeply hurt.

Certain themes come up often from every part of the world.

Love is powerful.

People aren't predictable.

Too often they aren't kind.

Healing takes time.

Moving on is liberating.

Finding love starts with loving yourself first.

I have received nearly 10,000 submissions from 117 countries.

Telling your story and baring your soul is never easy. I am beyond grateful for the courage of everyone who has taken the time to be a part of this.

This book is a raw, often painful account of modern day romance, told through the voices of those who have experienced it firsthand.

beginning

Tell me something about you.
The worst thing about you.
The thing that could make me hate you.

Tell me what you do when someone gets you angry.
Do you smash the things around you?
Or do you act very calm?

Tell me what you think about nature.
Would you rather stay at home?
Or make a wish while
looking at a falling star?

Tell me what you think about art.
Do you think it's a freaking mess?
Do you think it's silly?
Or is it the definition of the universe?

Tell me what you think about yourself.
Please don't lie to me.
I want to know the truth.
I want to know you, who you really are.

I want to know your opinion about the world.
War, humanity, existence.
I just want to know . . . all of this.

Female. Moldova.

I met this guy on Tinder and decided to give him a chance.

He picked me up from my house around 8:00 p.m. and took me out to a really nice restaurant. We stayed for about an hour, then went back to his apartment.

The entire time we were at his house all he talked about was video games. I finally had enough and started to leave.

He apologized and ended up persuading me to stay longer. We watched a movie and sat and chatted for a good while.

Later on, he went into the bathroom, and came back out completely naked and asked, "Are ya ready?"

I went completely silent, got my stuff to leave, and walked out.

Once I got downstairs, I called my best friend to come get me. To this day I still have him blocked and haven't spoken a word to him since.

Female. Massachusetts.

Every day I wait to talk to you.
Every day I wait to be with you.
Every day my mind hurts from thinking about you so much.
Every day I smile just thinking about you.
Every day I want to tell you I love you.
Every night I dream about the softness of your lips.
Every night I can't sleep because of the anticipation that each day leads me closer to being with you.

Female. New York.

We had already slept together twice, before telling me over drinks that he had a girlfriend, and he was seeing me just for sex.

I was really angry, didn't know what to do, and I had to think quickly.

I decided to get payback.

After we finished our drinks I agreed to go back to his place. I acted very calm and cool.

Once there, we started making out, and I recommended we make it interesting. He was curious, and he agreed. I proceeded to use his socks to tie him up very tightly to his bedpost. He couldn't move—and he was loving it!

Next, I completely undressed him. He was totally naked, with no blanket over him, and was still unable to move.

He then watched as I collected my things, and got ready to leave the apartment.

He became enraged and kept asking why I was doing this.

I told him, "Don't hate the player, hate the game," and left the apartment.

I later found out through a mutual friend he was tied up all night and wasn't able to get untied until his roommate came home and found him the next morning.

Female. New York.

To my crush,

You make me so happy. When I see a text message from you my heart skips a beat.

When we talk I enter another universe with you. Your voice is my drug.

I think I'm falling for you.

Yesterday you asked me to be your girlfriend, and I couldn't have been happier, yet I didn't give you an answer.

I'm afraid. Everything seems so perfect with you, but I've been through a lot and I don't want to end up getting hurt as always.

I worry. About our time difference, and the fact that we live in different countries.

I'm scared. That you'll turn out to be like the others, that you will change with time, maybe get bored and leave.

I think these thoughts every night before I sleep.

Everything seems too good to be true, and I'm wondering what the catch is this time.

Female. Lebanon.

I met this guy at a club last week. We were getting along just fine, but when I tried to get his number he would always change the subject.

So I got him just a bit drunk and figured that he would tell me.

Seeing as he still wouldn't, I followed him to his apartment, which turned out to be in the building next to mine!

Now I'm dying to see him but I'm just too embarrassed.

Female. Texas.

I started dating this one guy who was super hot, and pretty funny.
He was a "bad boy," so pretty much my type.

We were talking a lot, and I started to really like him.

He would send me good morning and goodnight texts, and always told me how beautiful I was to him.

After about four months, his personality changed. He became more angry and distant, and seemed to hate the world.

He started wearing a lot of black, and even started painting his nails and wearing eyeliner. When I would ask if anything was wrong, he always said no.

He invited me to go to his house for dinner. I agreed even though I was skeptical of his behavior.

I got to his house, and as soon as I walked in, there were pentagrams and other satanic symbols everywhere.

He told me he was a Satanist and that he wanted to sacrifice me to Satan, so he would be granted high power.

Needless to say, I ran out of the house, blocked him on everything, and never heard from him again.

Female. Nebraska.

I liked her since the moment I saw her.
She was smart, pretty, funny, friendly,
and I always wanted to get to know her better.

I moved away, and finally told her what she means to me.
She said she was flattered but didn't feel the same.

We continued talking for about a year, and when I hinted at meeting up,
she declined. I discovered she was seeing another guy.

I had no reason to be jealous but it still hurt. Over the year
we had been talking, my feelings had only deepened and grown.

"About 3 months, I think" were the exact words she used to describe
how long she had been seeing the other guy.

He had achieved in three months what I had failed to do in five years.

He took her heart, and she's still got mine.

Male. UK.

I went on a blind date with a guy to a pizza place. He insisted we each get our own personal pizzas.

At the end of the date he "forgot his wallet" and asked me to pay.

He didn't have a car, and as I was dropping him off, he snatched both of our leftover pizzas and ran.

Female. West Virginia.

I met this girl at a party and our conversation got off to a good start. I felt something for her, and I thought she did also.

I knew her for about a year, before she met my older brother. I was jealous, and it would hurt to see them talking.

One day she texted me, "I love you."

But then she texted me saying, "Sorry, wrong person, it was meant for your brother."

I broke down in tears every night, wondering how she could do that to me. I know they are still talking, while I'm just sitting here alone in the corner.

Male. Belgium.

My best friend has been in jail for almost a year.

He sort of just stopped talking to me after he got arrested.

Then out of the blue one day he contacted me, and we started
writing letters back and forth. The letters turned into phone calls.

He told me that he's had feelings for me since the day we met.

I started to realize that I actually really like him. It scares me.

We aren't even in the same state anymore,
but I would move to be closer to him in a heartbeat.

Female. Oregon.

Our first date was a picnic in the park. While I was skeptical about his deep-seated interest in astrology, in some ways we were perhaps too similar; I went home thinking, "I have found the male version of me."

We had a second date, after which he invited me to his place for a dinner date the following evening. The food was great; I was starting to really like this guy.

After dinner, he walked me back home, and I offered for him to come upstairs. We were getting closer, and having that awkward chat just before you kiss. We started discussing good restaurants in the area. I suggested he check out a local bakery—to which his response was, "Yeah, I've checked out their dumpster before." Slightly bewildered, I asked him to repeat what he meant.

"I'm into dumpster diving. I used to lead tours of the different dumpsters in the area. You can get all sorts of things, from bread, to groceries, to fish heads for soups—all for free, just because the restaurants decided to throw them away."

I was stunned, and followed up by asking, "What about the food you served me tonight? Any of that come from one of your dumpster dives?" He began to smirk and I immediately realized I knew the answer. I felt sick.

I knew it was over, and I told him, "I think it's time to go home." As soon as he left, I went directly to the bathroom to brush my teeth and shower. With all the scrubbing I did, I still did not feel clean.

Female. New York.

Completely fell in love.
Head over heels.
Can't eat.
Can only think and dream of him.

He's an unhappily married man.

I just can't be another woman though, I want to be the only woman.

Female. Los Angeles.

I went on a first date since my ex and I broke up.

This guy was very sweet at first, but then he just started acting really weird.

I would get random calls and texts from him saying he's happy he got to see me today, even though I hadn't seen him in about a week.

Then he started sending me photos he had taken of me.

These pictures included ones of me in my room, and in my house. They were taken from quite a distance away with the camera zoomed in.

I blocked his number and blocked him on all social media. I called the cops, got a restraining order, and never heard from him again.

Female. Illinois.

I didn't know hatred could turn into love;
I thought that was only in the movies.

I met this guy three years ago, didn't like him at first, but in the passing spirals of time I realized that I was head over heels in love with him.

Little arguments and beautiful talks.

He fails to understand the worth that I see in him. He fails to see that other girls won't understand him the way I do.

He's dated two or three girls since I started liking him.

I won't call him my friend, because heaven knows, we look at each other just a little too long to be just friends.

But the fact is, guys like him don't fall for girls like me.

I wish I could tell him that he's made me fall in love with every single bit of him.

But ultimately, I know his happiness won't be with me.

Female. Canada.

He took me to a Chinese restaurant because I'm Asian
and he said he wanted to do something special and authentic for me.
Yes really.

Female. Washington.

I was in love with my best friend for four years, and she knew it.

She wanted to give it a go after all that time,
and we spent the night at her place.

The next day, she told me she didn't feel right
and never spoke to me ever again.

Years of friendship wasted over one night of passion.

Female. Scotland.

We both secretly love one another but are too afraid
to make the first move.

Maybe it's the fear of objection by our families, or maybe we are afraid
that we won't last.

It's all too good to be true. Late night texts, and unwavering support, it
just hurts to give up this precious chance.

We could be the happiest couple, but because I am a coward, nothing has
ever happened between us, and this will be the greatest regret I ever have.

Male. Malaysia.

My boyfriend and I have only been together for a couple of weeks.

He gave me the password to his phone, and I looked through his messages.

He has been texting with this girl.
She was writing things like, "I love you baby."

It upset me, and when I confronted him he denied there was anything going on and said "Nah, she's like a sister to me."

Female. Arizona.

We met on Tinder.

He told me he had moved from France to Mexico to live with his now ex-girlfriend, which was interesting because I had also moved to Mexico to be with my now ex-boyfriend.

We went on a date with our dogs, drank wine, and then hooked up at his place.

He invited me to stay with him for the weekend, and I accepted.

His bathroom was still full of his ex's things.

When I was leaving, I suggested he move on and throw away her stuff (tampons and make up), and he confessed that they actually were still dating and live together.

He went on Tinder because his girlfriend was traveling for the weekend and he didn't want to be alone.

Female. Mexico.

Dude.

It's the only word I've been able to call you for three years.

I want to call you mine.

Other people just think of you as strange and off-putting, but I see more and know how amazing you are.

I can't believe you make me feel this way, but I love you, though I bet you'll never hear it from my lips.

Male. Louisiana.

I was on a blind date with a really nice girl.

It was one of those nights where everything clicked, and we ended up having sex that night.

Right after we had sex she started talking about babies and marriage.

I froze because I hadn't used a condom.

Male. Sweden.

I used to think he was so stuck up, but then I got to know him.

I fell in love with him really quickly.

We had an amazing Christmas together, yet I still hadn't told him how I felt.

I was able to finally gather the courage one night, but before I said a word he told me he didn't want anything to happen.

I used to do everything for him. He had nothing and I gave him everything.

Now he's dating some whore, and he's going to get hurt.

Still though, if he wanted to be with me right now,
I'd be with him in a heartbeat.

Female. UK.

We met, and then the texting started.
We had a lot in common, and when I asked her out, she said yes.

On our first date we just sat and talked for four hours. It was amazing.

We were dating for a month, and her replies to my messages started to slow down.

I asked her if she thought she might not be able to handle this relationship.

She told me that she didn't realize we were even dating, and thought we were just friends all along.

Male. Israel.

My mistake wasn't falling in love with you.

My mistake was thinking that one day you would fall in love with me also.

Female. Nevada.

My girlfriend can be really unaffectionate at times.
I understand, and I respect the fact that she expresses her love differently, which is something I have to get used to.

She's just generally not a touchy-feely person, and it hurts sometimes not being able to do the things you'd look forward to doing. I wish I could hold her by the waist, kiss for a bit longer, be more intimate, and grow closer.

It makes me feel rejected, and scared. It hurts most when others tell you that you deserve better, even when you know they're wrong.

I have to figure out a way through this. I love her and I don't want to let her go, she means too much to me. I must find a way to adjust to how she wants to be affectionate.

I know I probably won't get more than I already have, she's even said so. This is why I know I am the one who must adjust.

Male. Kansas.

At a young age I decided love wasn't for me.

I would look to the stars and ask to meet someone,
but it wasn't happening.

I joined the Army and instantly became friends with a beautiful woman.
She was engaged so I wanted to respect that.

Later she told me they were on a break, and within two weeks we fell in love.

I've never felt so happy in my life. I don't deserve her, but one day I hope
she'll realize how much she truly means to me.

I'm hoping she'll marry me! She would be my first and my last.

Male. Missouri.

uncertainty

I've noticed you aren't holding me as tightly anymore.

Your smile isn't there after we kiss.

You don't pull me back for another hug before I leave.

You aren't the same.

I can feel you slowly leaving, and it's so difficult because the thought of not having you makes me cry.

Please, please don't go.
Please explain what's happened.
Please let's get back to where we once were.

Female. Florida.

She is my best friend, and I've always been in love with her.

Recently she took me up to this place we call "our spot."

She told me she was head over heels for me and that someday she is going to marry me, but right now she can't be with me because she has to find herself.

She needs to love herself before she can love anyone else, and I understand that.

I watch her flirt and date other people, while telling me they don't mean anything to her.

I haven't been dating anyone, and I know that's my choice. But I think it's unfair for her to date other people if she is in love with me.

I know I should probably just give up hope and stop waiting. It's just hard.

Female. New Mexico.

She was dating one of my best friends who would hurt her, cheat on her, and hit her.

She finally broke it off, and two years later we reconnected at a club.

I give her all the attention in the world. I love her, and she said she loves me too.

But even she agrees that she doesn't give me the attention I deserve. I don't need much, but cuddle me, hold me, be by my side when I need you most.

We laugh, we smile, have great memories, and I told her we should move in together, and start our lives as a couple.

We've been together for one year. I know I'm in love with her, but I have a feeling she's not in love with me.

I want to keep fighting and not give up. She's the reason I wake up every morning with a smile on my face, and go to sleep every night the same way.

I'm not sure what to do.

How do I know she really loves me?
How do I know a year from now she will be by my side?

Male. Florida.

I am in love and engaged to a wonderful man.

However, I have yet to introduce him to my racist father.

It's a very sad situation because my fiancé happens to be
Muslim. I am afraid at the wedding my dad will offend
his family, as he did to someone I dated before.

I don't know what the future will bring and it frightens me as neither
myself nor my mother can control my father's words or hate.

Female. Canada.

We recently travelled to meet my boyfriend's family for the first time
after being together for almost two years.

At a family BBQ, his eight-year-old nephew bluntly said that his uncle will
never marry me, because it's already been a while and he hasn't asked yet.

I brought this up to my boyfriend, and he said it's not that he doesn't
want to marry me, he just doesn't think about marriage as often as I do.

I had made it clear from the beginning that
I'm dating to find a life partner and get married.

I told him I want to end the relationship. He said he needed
a year and a half more time to be ready for marriage.

He doesn't want to let me go, and does actually seem to want to marry me.

He's nervous, not about life with me, but about losing his independence.

Female. New York.

We have been dating on and off for three years.

We are different nationalities, have different religions, and our parents are not okay with us being together.

We both are getting older, and I want to spend the rest of my life with her.

I am just afraid to ask her to get married. Both of our families are religious, and almost certainly won't support us getting married.

I truly don't know whether we should sacrifice our love for the sake of our parents, or ignore all of that and just get married.

Male. Qatar.

I've been crazy about her since the day we met.

She lives in Detroit and works 100-hour weeks, so I rarely get to see her and usually by the end of the week we barely get to talk.

We had a date on Monday and in my drunkenness I let it slip that I love her. She said she loved me too.

Now she hasn't texted me back in more than forty-eight hours.

This is my first relationship in two years since I broke up with a girl I dated for eight years. I'm anxious and insecure, and scared she is going to disappear on me.

She's always sorry for not texting me back right away. I just wish I could know it's going to be okay.

I'm just broken from my past, I never trust anyone. I'm always second guessing. I don't believe anything. It hurts.

Male. Illinois.

We dated for four months. I got pregnant.

We stayed together for two years, even though things were rocky.

His struggles to keep a job made us very financially unstable. On top of that, my family dislikes him, and this caused a lot of issues.

We broke up and got back together twice.

We had just started to rekindle things for a third time when I found out he slept with someone else and then lied to me about it.

He's the father of my child and I love him more than I thought I ever could love someone. But I just don't know if I can look past all of this.

Female. Canada.

An old girlfriend reached out recently, and told me she loved me.

I am currently dating someone else, and normally I would have just told her that.

The problem is that my ex has already told her dad she still has these feelings for me . . . and her dad is my uncle.

That's right. I dated my stepcousin.

I'm not sure what to do, but I'm worried about having to deal with my uncle.

Male. Hawaii.

The first year we dated I kept catching my boyfriend
talking with girls on different dating sites.

Finally he told me the reason was because he suspected
I was cheating on him with my ex. I wasn't.

Once I cut all ties with my ex, I never caught
my boyfriend doing anything like that again.

We got married about a year later and it's been great.

I can't help but still be paranoid even though we've been married
for two years. What happens the next time he gets insecure?

I constantly wait until he's asleep and look through his phone.
I check his accounts, emails, messages, and I don't find a thing.

I'm constantly questioning him when he works late and have
even driven by a few times to make sure he was actually working.

I married him thinking I was past this, but I guess I wasn't. He
messaged an old friend saying, "Hey, how are you?" and I flipped out.

I'm truly not sure how to get beyond this constant paranoia.

Female. Florida.

We were so young, and he was so cute and sweet. I was in love.

We got engaged, and have now been together for seven years.

He is twenty-four now, but he never grew up and stopped being that cute boy. He never acts like a man when things get tough.

I have to handle everything.

Three months ago I started talking with another guy, someone who is super mature.

I am starting to fall in love with this guy, but after all these years I don't want to hurt my boyfriend.

I don't want to break up. Deep down I believe that my boyfriend will grow up some day and act like an adult. Everything might be perfect again.

But I can't stop thinking about this other guy. He makes me feel like a woman. He makes me feel secure.

Female. Greece.

We've been together for over a year.

We started as "exclusive friends with benefits," which I thought was pretty much dating anyway.

When he said he wanted to make it official I was so happy.

He later told me he wanted to sleep with other girls also. "Not too often," he said, "only when I feel like it."

How did we go backwards? I just want him all to myself.

Female. Indiana.

I'm dating a younger guy who has a three-year-old daughter with another woman.

When we first met neither of us were looking for a relationship, but we fell in love no matter how hard we tried not to.

His ex-girlfriend is psycho, and uses their daughter as a way to punish him.

She was at the house one day, and found out we were dating by going through his dirty laundry and finding my panties (which she stole).

She then proceeded to not let him see his daughter for eight weeks because he was dating me.

I feel so bad that because of me he can't see his daughter. Sometimes I feel like I should end this relationship so he can see her.

I'm afraid that one day he will resent me for being the reason he can't see his daughter.

I'm just head over heels for him and hate seeing him hurting.

Female. Oregon.

I fell in love during my senior year of college.
After two years of dating, he proposed, and I said yes.

Eventually he started acting differently, and I knew something was up.

One night when he was asleep his phone kept going off, so I went to turn it off and found out that he was cheating on me with an eighteen-year-old girl who wasn't even in college yet.

I confronted him, he admitted to it, and apologized.

He said it's entirely my choice if I still want to marry him.

Female. Minnesota.

My boyfriend of three years wants to experiment with sex toys
and is finding ways to ask me to be more promiscuous.

I am not as interested in sex as he is and I feel like I'm holding him back.

He always says that he wished he had more sexual experiences, and if he
was single now, he would be sleeping with a lot of women.

He is honest and I don't think he will ever cheat, but I feel so insecure
and upset that I'm not enough for him.

Female. Delaware.

I love my husband like a best friend and we seem "perfect."

Safe. Vanilla. Boring, to say the least.

Before I met my husband, I was in love with another man. We are still best friends and love each other. We can't resist one another and lately we've gotten more comfortable than ever. I'm in love with him completely and he knows it. We both want to know what it would be like to be together.

I'm scared I married my husband because it was "safe" and was what our families wanted.

Every time I look at the other guy, my heart melts.

I'm contemplating divorce but I'm uncertain because we have been together for so long and it's still early in our marriage.

Female. Florida.

My boyfriend and I have been together for four months now.

We are both totally in love, but I only recently discovered that he is asexual.

I know this will make the relationship very hard for me to be in.

I also know it would crush him if I broke up with him.

Male. UK.

I have been with my boyfriend for almost a year.
I love him beyond what any words could describe.

I trust him with my life and I know he loves me just as much.

I've messed up majorly in my past, and he needs to know about it.
It's a really hard subject for me to bring up. No one knows about it.

He knows I'm hiding something, but doesn't know what it is, and he
doesn't ever question it.

I'm scared if I tell him, he will see me differently. I'm not sure what to do.

Female. Australia.

I've been dating this girl for a year and we kept our relationship secret.
She didn't want to come out, and I loved her, so I stayed and waited.

She eventually told some people, but we are still mostly a secret.
She hasn't told her parents, and doesn't bring me around to see
her friends very often.

She doesn't post pictures of me, and it bothers me. I feel like I'm not
even in a relationship sometimes.

I love her so much, but I get overwhelmed with this feeling that I'm not
good enough for her.

I don't know what to do. The pain kills me, and we argue often about this.

I feel insecure and that she's always looking for a way out.

I don't want to break up with her but it hurts either way.

Female. Rhode Island.

cheating

My boyfriend and I were together for about nine months.

We were so in love, and I thought he was the one I would spend the rest of my life with.

We talked about our wedding, and decided to get married after I graduate from university.

The day before we planned to look at houses, he sent me a text telling me how sorry he was, but he can't do it anymore.

He had been dating some other girl for quite some time.

He broke up with me over text!

I am still really upset and heartbroken. I can't get over him.

Female. Singapore.

I'm in a long-distance relationship with this amazing guy,
but I've cheated on him four times.

I know I sound like a total whore right now, but I know I will never ever do that again. I regret my behavior, and have changed.

He forgave me even though he shouldn't have.

They say a cheater is always a cheater; I'm not sure if that's true.

I want to change, I'm determined to change.

I know he will be my husband one day, and I need to earn his trust.

Female. California.

We met in college while she was dating someone else,
yet we fell in love anyway.

She was a free spirit. I loved that about her, but I let her get away.

She popped up six years later. She was married, had a kid,
and she was now very sick.

We were still in love.

She told me she was unhappy and getting a divorce soon.
For the next year we saw each other whenever possible.

The highs were high, and the lows were low.

It felt wrong being with a married woman, but she was the one I had
been waiting for all my life.

Her husband found out about us and things got bad.
He refused to sign the divorce papers.

I got her pregnant, but I was not ready to have a child.
She wanted to keep it. The child died stillborn.

He texted me one day "she is MY WIFE! Not yours!"

It was all too much. I let her go.

Male. Florida.

My boyfriend and I were spending the night out at separate pubs.

Later in the evening I drove to a friend's house. I knocked and rang the doorbell, but then I remembered that she told me to come in because the door was unlocked.

Then I heard them. My boyfriend and my friend were in the kitchen having sex.

She asked me if I wanted to have a threesome.

I told her to go fuck herself and left.

I got all my boyfriend's things from my place, put them in a bag, and left it outside.

I never spoke to either of them again.

Female. Ireland.

I met a girl when I was much younger, and we dated for five years.

I used to buy her flowers every week and call her my princess.
I used to call her and say, "Good morning baby girl, have a wonderful
day!" Before she would hang up I would kiss my phone.

A year ago I was diagnosed with cancer, and at around
the same time she slept with my best friend.

Today I am single, cancer-free, and I've never been so depressed.

I'm shocked by the amount of people that want to have meaningless sex.

It makes me feel like garbage.

I recently went out with a girl I had just met.
I got her flowers, and she called me pathetic.

All I've ever wanted was to make a girl feel special.

Male. Canada.

My girlfriend took a trip to visit her best friend who had moved away.

I knew something was up when I saw the way her best friend's brother had his arm on her leg in a picture.

But of course when I confronted her, she called me crazy, and added that he was engaged. I loved this girl and trusted her.

After she got back home, I noticed her acting a little funny. I later found out that same guy had flown here to visit her, and they had sex in a hotel.

She broke my heart.

Male. New York.

I met this older guy, but at the time I had a boyfriend.

He called me and we went out. A bad boy with nice abs.

I gave my virginity to him by the third date.

I was sneaking over to his house at least twice a week;
we would drink and have sex.

It was all so wrong and secretive. That was the appeal.

Female. California.

We were dating for a year and a half.

I am in the military and was deployed for a nine-month tour.

A month after I left, she told me she was going out with some girlfriends, but I found out she had actually hung out with a guy.

I didn't talk to her for a couple days, but I then forgave her.

A month later she stopped talking to me.

I kept sending texts and calling her but got no response. Then she sent me a text to break up with me.

She called me a week later and said she had been sleeping with someone else for a while. Her excuse? She was lonely.

Male. Texas.

I was working at the restaurant, about to close down the dining room.

As I was wiping down the tables, this guy walked in and placed an order. He said he forgot his wallet, so he went home to get it.

While he was gone, my boyfriend had come in to break up with me.

After my boyfriend left, the guy came back, and saw me in tears. He was comforting me, but I reassured him everything would be okay.

We exchanged numbers and started hanging out as friends. A few months passed, and on Christmas he took me out, gave me a present, and kissed me.

We started dating and were together for four months, and I lost my virginity to him. It turns out he was cheating on me the whole time we were together.

When I was at work, he was at her house.

He wasn't even the one who told me about her—it was his best friend, who broke up with me for my boyfriend because he was too cowardly to do it himself.

Female. Illinois.

I confessed to my boyfriend that I had sex with my ex
after I was devastated that my pet died.

He said he forgave me and asked me to never do it again. He said he was
hurt but told me not to worry about it, and went back to his normal self.
He told me he won't leave me just as long as I don't cheat again.

He took my cheating really lightly though, and that's what scares me.

Female. California.

I was in a long-distance relationship with this girl
for about four months after being best friends for years.

After a while, things got rocky.

A few days before we broke up, she went to a party and posted pictures
of herself making out with a guy.

I was so sad and angry that I did the very same thing.

A whole year later I realized she had been logged into my Facebook and
Google accounts since we broke up, and was able to see everything.

Male. Sweden.

I was so in love with him, and I thought he felt the same.

I found out he sent nude photos to nine different girls, and cheated on me with them all.

Female. UK.

I cheated on my boyfriend countless times.

I kept it from him till someone I used to trust
betrayed me and told him what I did.

My boyfriend wanted to know if it was true,
and said he'd take me back once he knew the real truth.

I told him the truth, but a week later, he said he
lost all feelings for me and broke up with me.

We agreed to stay friends, but it hurts to not call him mine anymore.

Female. Singapore.

I went to a hotel with my mum for a spa day,
and ran into my boyfriend of four years.

He had told me he was going to be out with his friends shopping,
but instead he was with my best friend.

He said, "Sorry, I'm dating her, oops."

He then dumped me right there in front of my mum.

A week later he texted me saying he wanted me back and he's sorry.

I blocked him.

Female. UK.

I recently broke up with my boyfriend when I discovered he was dating my best friend being my back. I also found out he had slept with another girl when we were together as well.

I was furious.

I called his boss and made up a fake story.

Long story short, he no longer has a job.

Female. UK.

I met my soul mate almost five years ago.

We hit it off from the start. We were on and off for a while but eventually became official and I was the happiest I've ever been in my life.

After about a year, things started getting rocky. We were fighting a lot and we always kind of just pushed our issues to the back burner.

I broke up with him six months ago.

He has a new girlfriend now, but when she's not around, he tells me he will always love me and cheats on her with me.

I know I should feel bad about all of this, but I don't.

Female. New York.

I dated this guy for almost a year.

We had already gone through the whole "I love you" thing by this point.

I had asked him one day why he never moaned my name during sex. His excuse was that my name was too long to moan . . .

He apparently also cheated on me the entire time.

Female. California.

We dated for eight months, on and off, but I thought he was my forever.

One day I found out he was cheating on me with the mother of his child. I stayed quiet and kept my feelings to myself.

While he lay next to her at night in bed, I lay alone on the bathroom floor because it was me who had a miscarriage.

I didn't want to mess up their family, but I often think about the family we could have been.

Female. Illinois.

I drank too much and ended up kissing the girl
you'd warned me about.

She never had good intentions. I didn't listen. I let my guard down and she kissed me.

I felt guilty about it so I did the right thing and told you. I cut ties with that other girl and tried to make it right with you.

You and I moved in together, we got engaged.

You gave back the ring a few months later, telling me you just couldn't get past the betrayal of that kiss.

I lost you. I regret what I did.

I wish you could see that I still love you.
I miss you every day.
I want you back.

How can I forgive myself for hurting you? And in turn ruining us?

Female. Arizona.

My ex decided to break up with me on our two-year anniversary because he didn't feel the same about me anymore.

I later found out he had cheated on me for a majority of the relationship with two of my "friends," one of which is a guy.

Long story short, I kicked my ex between the legs and I haven't talked to any of them since.

Female. Oregon.

She promised.
She lied.
She cheated.
She broke me.
She took everything I knew and made me forget it.
She took everything I fought for and burned it to the ground.
I gave up my life for her without realizing it was already gone.
When she was texting me, she was texting him.
And in the end, I guess I just wasn't good enough.

Male. New Jersey.

heartbreak

I will always be here for you,
she said, and then she left.

Male. Lebanon.

The man I love was in jail for seven months.

We wrote to each other the whole time he was away.

He convinced me he was falling in love with me, and that he wanted to date me. I decided to wait for him.

He was released five days ago.

I tried to contact and see him, and then found he went back to his ex-girlfriend.

I feel like I'll never believe it when someone says, "I love you," again.

Words mean nothing—actions do.

Female. Indiana.

During my first vacation to New York City I met a guy
at a bar and we instantly clicked.

My trip was short, but we got to hang out again the day before I went home.

It was the most amazing date of my life.

When I got home we barely talked but we would text each other to say how much it sucked that we lived so far away.

Last year, we started talking again, and he said he still felt the same way about me.

I just couldn't get him out of my head.

Blinded by my excitement, I bought a ticket to New York City, but once I was there he wouldn't answer my messages.

He later texted me saying he had just started a relationship and felt guilty for not telling me sooner.

So there I was, 3000 miles away from home, crying my eyes out for a fantasy that wasn't going to happen.

Male. Guatemala.

I'm still in love with you.

I cry thinking about falling asleep without your embrace.

About the days you will no longer come home to me.

Or the way you smell after you've just showered.

You have opened my mind to myself, and the love
I have to both give and receive.

You are the love of my life but I know you don't see a future with me.

Female. Washington.

I proposed to my girlfriend of two and a half years
in a bamboo forest in Maui.

She said yes! Then four months later, she gave me back the ring and told me she had changed her mind.

She let me announce our engagement to my entire family. I was humiliated when I had to tell them the wedding was cancelled.

She wants to be friends, but my heart is broken.

I still love her. I keep thinking she'll come back. I am still paying for the ring I had designed for her.

I continue to pretend to be her friend only because I want her in my life.

I miss her every day.

Female. Arizona.

We fell in love with the same person.

I loved her, and she loved herself.

I still haven't mustered up enough courage
to demand respect or walk away.

Female. North Carolina.

My husband left right after our daughter was born.

He hasn't talked to me since,
unless it's to fight and tell me how awful I am.

Female. Illinois.

He broke up with me three months ago,
but everything about him still haunts me.

His laugh.
His smile.
His way with words.

The way that he can make you feel like you're the only person he's ever
seen . . . but you're not. He makes everyone feel that way.

When you finally break down and tell him you're done, he twists and
mangles the story to benefit him. Only him.

He'll leave you with nothing.
He'll take everything that once belonged to you.
And watch as you apologize for his mistakes.

Female. Canada.

I met him at a bonfire at college towards the end of my freshman year. We started off as friends, but the chemistry was blatantly visible between the both of us.

We weren't out to each other though, and certainly not to anyone else for that matter.

The beginning of my junior year, late at night, we were chatting on text. We were heavily flirting, and he told me he was bisexual.

I told him I was curious, and he called me immediately. We talked for a while, and he told me he'd proudly call me his boyfriend. I was too scared and anxious to process anything but I knew I felt the same towards him.

We met up a couple weeks later. He stayed over. We talked. He told me he had kids.

Later I found out he was still married. Things got weird. I ended it. I haven't talked to him in years. He's working on his marriage.

I still think about him and wonder if he ever really cared about me.

Male. Michigan.

I texted him three times in a row.

My grandmother was on her deathbed and I needed him to be there for me.

He decided I was too clingy and that the best way to break up with me was to block me on all social media.

On the day my grandmother died.

Female. Texas.

I met her . . .
She was so gorgeous.
Light green eyes that made me feel so at home.

Her.

She and I dated for a full year.

Then

She began to build her future without me.
She began to distance me.
She began to ignore me.
She began to blame me.
She began to hurt me.

She broke up with me, cut me out of her life as if I didn't exist.

Then

She saw me doing better.
She started to see what she let go of.
She missed her chance.

And it's her fault.

Female. Namibia.

I was living in Leeds, England. It was my first time abroad,
and I knew I'd be living there at least a year.

I met a girl at a party. She asked me about my tattoos, and we joked
around. She looked at me from across the room a few more times
afterwards. She was beautiful.

We all left in different cars. We went to a nightclub, the kind you have to
talk your way into, even if you aren't special.

We both love dancing and hit the dance floor.

We danced together, we kissed, we made out, we left. A girl with a
British accent. Yeah, that'll do it.

We spent the night together. It was perfect.

I walked her back to her friend's.

We fell in love on our first date. I've still never had a better one.

Then we said goodbye several months later.

Time and place are powerful.

Saying goodbye ain't easy.

I still long for her. What a beautiful mess.

Male. Canada.

I met a guy through a mutual friend—but I lived in Denver, and he lived in California.

He flew me out twice to see him in California, and he also came to visit me in Denver. It was going really well, and I found a job in California. He expressed how excited he was that we were finally going to be in the same state.

As I was driving out to California during my move, we would talk and text, and I'd send pictures of my journey. We talked up until Vegas.

As soon as I left Vegas for the final part of the drive, he suddenly stopped picking up my calls and responding to my texts.

We had gone through eight months of long distance, and now that I was almost there, moving my life for him, silence.

A month of total silence went by before one day I saw that that he "liked" one of my photos on social media. Other than that, that was it.

Female. Colorado.

I married a foreigner; we have been together for almost five years.

We have a baby girl who is six months old.

He went back home for a visit, and since he left it's been very hard for me to reach him. He stopped taking care of us, and ignores my calls and messages.

I just found out he is starting to date someone in his country. I don't know what to do. I don't want my baby to grow up without a father.

I'm so confused and stressed.

I can't even pay my rent while he has left me and is playing around.

I love him, but I can't live this way.

Female. Indonesia.

We dated for about three years,
and despite our ups and downs we were really happy.

Then all of a sudden out of nowhere she stopped replying to texts,
stopped picking up calls, and wouldn't let me see her.

A few days later I went to her house and found that it was empty.

She had moved to a different city, and didn't tell me or even have the
courage to break up with me.

Male. New Zealand.

I broke up with you because my family didn't support our relationship and they were about to kill you.

I still love you and want to be with you.

I miss you so much. I am always wishing you were here with me.

Female. Saudi Arabia.

We were together for two years before breaking up for a month, to see what it was like to date other people.

We got back together and I found out I was pregnant, but it wasn't his.

He stuck around almost until she was born and then he left.

My baby girl is almost two months old. I want him to come back home, but he doesn't know how to be a father to a baby who is not his.

We had plans to get married, and were closer than anything I've ever experienced in the years we spent together.

I've been nothing without him. Seeing my baby every day breaks my heart.

I know he must be heartbroken also.

But I still want him in our life, I want him to be her father.

I just don't know how to convince him that by being in love with me, he could also fall in love with this beautiful child as well.

Female. Delaware.

Day 1
I remember when our eyes met for the first time. I thought they were the most beautiful thing I've ever seen.

Day 12
We started hanging out. Soon, our group outings turned into one-on-one activities. Not official dates, but close enough.

Day 47
I've started catching feelings for you. You're kind, smart, and caring. We have long discussions that last until late in the evening. Neither of us wants to say goodnight first.

Day 96
We faced our feelings for the first time. If I wasn't so shy, maybe something would have happened tonight.

Day 203
We've known each other for a while now. I've fallen in love. You make me believe the feeling is mutual.

Day 405
You've stayed at my house before, but tonight it was just you and I. We stayed up until 4am, and fell asleep side-by-side. I really love you.

Day 410
The last few weeks have been horrible. Do I still exist?

Today
You broke my heart.

Female. Canada.

I was tricked by life itself.

It sent me an angel
With a lover's heart
But the devil's mind.

It sent me the best and
the worst days of my life
In only one person.

You.

Female. Canada.

I met a guy in a club and after a few drinks he asked for my number. He was a 26-year-old police officer. We were talking every day and went out a dozen times.

He told me he really wanted to have a relationship with me.

One day I went over to his place to see a movie. During the movie I asked him to use the bathroom.

He started acting very strangely and made up excuses like, "It's really messy right now." Finally he agreed. The bathroom was upstairs, and when I got up there I heard a noise.

I got scared so I went back to the living room and told him what happened.

He said it was probably my imagination, and I believed him but I didn't go back.

A few weeks passed. I was out with a friend and I called him to see how he was doing. He told me he was at work so we only talked for a few minutes.

A little while after that I was walking by a coffee shop and I saw him with a little boy. I found out the kid was his son, and that was the noise I heard that night.

I was furious. He admitted that he wasn't planning on telling me that he had a kid or that he was divorced.

I never talked to him again.

Female. Greece.

I finally broke up with my ex after a year-long toxic relationship.

She went to my parents' house and told them
she was pregnant with my child.

After threats, crying, and lots of yelling,
she admitted that it was a lie and got out of my life.

Male. Canada.

We dated for a year and a half.

She was the greatest person I ever met. I have no regrets about spending every moment with her.

The day she told me that she was moving away, it became difficult for me. I cried for many nights.

We started to drift apart as her departure date came closer. Once she was gone we rarely talked.

Eventually she called me, reminiscing about our time together. I knew she was opening the door for another chance, but I decided it was best that we didn't date, and instead took the time to work on ourselves.

A few months later, she got engaged to someone else.

I'm happy for her, even though I still love her.

Male. California.

guilt

I am dating him,
but I am in love with his best friend.

Female. South Africa.

I've been in a serious relationship for almost four years.

When I first started going out with my boyfriend, I felt like I had won the lottery. He became my best friend and my entire world.

But time passes, and passion fades.

I started having feelings for another guy. I can't stop thinking about him, and I can't get him out of my mind.

He is the first and last thought I have every day. I hate myself for having feelings for another guy.

I know I'm having second thoughts because I'm not happy or satisfied in my relationship. I feel so guilty.

I feel really confused because I still love my boyfriend, I'm just not in love with him anymore.

It really bums me out; we had our whole future planned out, we decided on the names for our babies already.

It's so hard to accept that something you worked so hard on is no longer working out. We gave each other everything we had.

I can't believe my relationship is ending and it's because of me.

I don't think I will ever win another lottery.

Female. Canada.

One day at a party I hooked up with my best friend's girlfriend.

We were both pretty wasted, but I still feel bad about it.

He has no idea, and I really don't want him to know.

She has sent me very sexual messages since then,
and I'm not sure if I should just tell him.

Male. Pennsylvania.

He said he wasn't exactly married, that he married her to do her a favor.

We met again in person and things went from hot to naked. The sexual connection we had was unexplainable.

The next time I went to visit him, I got a hotel room and he stood me up.

I sent him a message later on to express how hurtful that was.

In the end, I liked him way more than I should have.

I am married also. I guess this is what karma feels like.

Female. California.

I met her online.

Slowly and quietly, I fell in love with her.

I fell in love with her words, her attitude, her kindness to others.

I fell in love with her pain and her happiness.

She was everything I wanted, except, she didn't know who I actually was.

She thought I was a guy who lived in the US, when in fact I was a girl in Jamaica.

We talked online for four years.

During those four years, she fell in love with me also, until the day she found out I was really a girl.

She forgave me, though she now saw me as someone else, and all those feelings vanished.

Female. Florida.

My partner and I share a house together.

I love him so much, he is my absolute world, and I can't wait to marry him one day.

But I've had this online thing with another guy.

It's nothing sexual, and we haven't even met yet, but I can't stop thinking about meeting him and seeing him.

It's not like I want to have sex with him, but I just feel this really strong need to just see him.

I figure if I see him maybe I'll stop thinking about him.

Female. UK.

I liked this guy, but he made me really angry.

I went psycho, tried to ruin his life, and told everyone lies about him.

I made up a whole story to get sympathy, even though the guy didn't really do much wrong.

I still really like the guy, but he doesn't trust me anymore.

Female. California.

I was a bad boyfriend.

She loved me with everything she had, and I cheated on her.

I hurt her so many times and she gave me another chance. I ruined that chance, and broke her heart yet again.

Now she is happily dating another guy.

I love her more than anything but now it is too late.

I was too dumb to understand what I was messing up.

Male. Croatia.

I've been with him for almost two years.

He is an amazing man, better than I could have even imagined.

But . . . There's always a 'but.'

I still love the guy I dated before him.
I constantly think about him, wonder where he is, what he's doing,
and if he's started dating someone else.

I have to stop myself from texting him and finding out for myself.

I don't know how to let myself forget him.

Female. Illinois.

I left a girl who I wasn't really in love with, and the same day I started dating someone else.

We are happy, and are totally in love with each other.

Am I a horrible person? How messed up am I?

I tried to love her, I really did.

Sometimes I lie awake at night thinking that I ruined that girl's life.

Male. Georgia.

I recently started seeing this guy I've known for a long time.

The problem is I'm married and he's in a serious relationship.

I've cheated before but my husband forgave me (he doesn't know how far things went).

Sometimes I wish I was single, but I don't want to be the one filing for divorce.

We have three kids and I feel like I'm being selfish when I think about divorce.

But at the same time I would like to have the freedom to do as I please.

I love my husband, we have been married for more than ten years, and he doesn't deserve this.

However, I enjoy this new guy's company and it seems we're starting to catch feelings for each other.

Female. California.

I dated a guy on and off long distance for many years.

It had its ups and downs. When it was good it was great, when it was bad it was terrible.

We both have moved on and I've been dating another guy for seven years.

Somehow my ex and I always seem to contact each other.

We do it as friends, but I always wonder *what if*, and I feel so guilty because my current boyfriend is an amazing man.

Female. New York.

I'm married and am seeing someone else.

He lives in another state and is recently divorced.

He has started to date other people and it's really bothering me.

Not sure what is wrong with me since I'm the one who is married.

Female. North Carolina.

I'm studying in India and my boyfriend
is in Singapore pursuing his masters.

It's been only three months that we have been apart.

I haven't cheated on him yet, but I am thinking a
lot these days about having sex with other guys.

I can't control this feeling.

Female. India.

I've been in a relationship for a year now.

I'm very happy, but I don't get to see him much anymore. At the end of the day, he is the man I intend to marry.

I recently got a new job and there's a guy I work with that I'm developing feelings for.

He's really handsome with pretty eyes and a nice smile. He's a bit of a jerk but has a warm heart.

I'm very attracted to him, and I'm not sure, but I think he might have feelings for me as well.

If he does, I would want him to act on it and it can be our little secret.

It can be a casual no-strings-attached relationship.

Just two lonely people who want some affection.

Female. Indiana.

pain

I met a guy online.

He was a year older than me, and I thought I was in love.
I mean, I was young. I didn't understand the ways people
can abuse you in a relationship.

It was okay in the beginning, but then he started controlling me.
He isolated me from my friends, and I started cutting (again).

He fucked me up mentally and made me hate myself.

I don't love him anymore. I'm moving on.
I haven't dated anyone since, but I'm trying.

I'm just scared.

Male. Georgia.

My fiancé broke up with me because I was "emotionally unstable."

He knew that I had been drugged and raped,
and because of that I didn't want him to touch me.

One night he was very angry that I wouldn't have sex with him,
so he forced me.

His 250-pound body was double the size of mine.
He laid on top of me, and I couldn't move.

I kicked and screamed.

I was naive and stupid, I believed him when he said
he wouldn't do it again.

He did it again.

I called the police and told his family. He is now in jail.

Female. Rhode Island.

We dated for four years—my love for him was pure.

He cheated on me many times, but I always forgave him.

A few days ago, he slapped me, and hit me so hard that blood spilled out from my mouth and nose.

My dreams with him vanished in an instant.

He lost all my respect.

He is not the one I'm searching for in a soul mate.

He apologized, but my heart does not want to forgive him again.

I am not sure if I will ever be able to trust a guy again.

Female. India.

I fell in love with my best friend.

We had so many beautiful memories together.

He left me just before our one-year anniversary, and told me we should just be friends.

Some time passed, and I ran into him.

We went to our favorite place and talked under the stars.

I held his precious, shaking body and he told me he was a drug addict, and that's the real reason he broke up with me.

All I could do was cry, while he attempted to wipe my tears.

I want to help him, but he refuses to let me get close. There isn't a day that goes by that I don't think of saving him.

Female. Tennessee.

He was my mistake . . . He never should have happened.

He is the father of my son's best friend.

He used me.
I let him.

Now I can't look in the mirror at myself anymore. All I see are all the things wrong with me.

I can barely look at the person who I still love even though we didn't work.

All I see are those eyes of someone who used me.
All I see is disgust.

He destroyed me in his own way.
I helped him with the destruction.

Female. Arizona.

I don't know why I love him.

He uses me, plays with my emotions, and controls me.

Even though he does this, whenever my phone rings I hope I hear his voice.

I find myself waiting all day for a text that I'm never going to receive.

I feel lost and alone.

He's the only one in a long time that has made me feel like I'm not a total waste of space.

I feel like I'm always about to cry.

Female. Costa Rica.

He cheated on his girlfriend with me.

We dated for a year and a half. He was emotionally abusive and controlling, but I didn't realize until afterward.

He told all my friends that I'm a terrible person, and now I have nobody.

It's been eight months since we broke up and I still don't know how to handle it.

Female. Canada.

I've been with my boyfriend for five years now.

I know he loves me, but when he's angry he verbally abuses me a lot.

He says the meanest things, calls me a whore, and it breaks my heart.

Female. Pakistan.

I just found out I'm pregnant.

My now ex-boyfriend is mad that I want to keep the baby.

He keeps making me feel bad about this decision I'm making, and saying hurtful things while I'm just trying to be nice to him.

I want his support. I want him to be by my side and help me, but it seems like he wants no part of this.

I'm hurt and alone.

Female. Arizona.

We love each other madly, but
we both become very abusive during arguments.

I don't understand why we are so violent and become such horrible monsters
to each other even though we know that we would die for one another.

I hope we are able to find a way to stop doing this.

Female. France.

When I met him, I was so happy.
Happy to find a man that loved me as much as I loved him.

But months went by, and the beatings began.

It started with a slap to the chin, but then the fists came,
and the kicks to my body.

But nothing hurt worse than his words piercing
through my ears that ultimately broke my spirit.

Female. Sweden.

I was raped.

You found out.

You left.

I'm better off without you
but I can't help but feel pain.

Female. Canada.

We were friends for a while. I have always cared for him,
and eventually we started dating.

However, he has relapsed back into his alcoholism.
When he drinks, he's so mean and incoherent.

I see so much potential in him, and I want him to see it too.

I know he loves me, but the alcohol is not only hurting him,
it is breaking me.

He is amazing sober.

I am afraid that if I leave him he will totally lose control and his alcoholism
will get worse.

Female. Florida.

He abused me.

Mentally—telling me no one would ever love me other than him.
Sexually—even when I said no.
Monetarily—he didn't work.

I finally got the courage to leave him, realizing I would rather be alone than with someone like that.

Fast forward two years later and a guy stumbles into my life. He's not my usual type, we are so different.

I never knew I could actually love someone like this until I met him.

But, he's going through some tough times and I'm having to pay for everything once again.

Part of my subconscious is starting to feel taken advantage of and the other part of me is thinking I'm trying to self-sabotage, because I'm afraid it will turn into what my last relationship was.

He truly is working hard and not just sitting around using my money.

I'm having a hard time not ruining this though, maybe I feel like I don't deserve him.

Female. Oregon.

I feel so alone in my life.

I met this girl online, and I knew she wasn't really
who she said she was, but I didn't care.

I spent a year and a half talking to her.

I didn't want to feel so alone, so I just let this fake
person catfish me so I could at least have someone.

Male. New York.

I have been married for three years, but I am miserable.

I married into a very big family, and I feel like I'm a prisoner in this relationship.

I want to live my own life.

I want freedom, I just don't know how to get it.

Female. Washington.

I married my long-term boyfriend
and have now been married for two years.

He has no time for me, but when his friends call he is always ready to go out.

He never goes out with me, though. We have not even gone on our honeymoon.

We often fight. There is no love left between us.

I think we should get divorced.

Female. India.

The only problem in our relationship is that he's never had to deal with depression or anxiety before, and I have severe versions of both.

Every time I try to talk to him about what's bothering me, he just shuts down or gets uncomfortable.

I don't want to lose him because I can't handle my own stuff.

It's been a year, and I'm terrified one day he won't be able to take it anymore no matter how much he loves me.

Every day I'm terrified he's going to end it with me.

Female. Indiana.

I've been dating this guy for a while,
and he knows that my past boyfriend was abusive,
which causes me to have panic attacks because of my PTSD.

He is so sweet, and treats me better than I ever thought someone would,
but when I have these attacks I get so scared.

When I have an attack he walks away, trying not to hurt or scare me
more, but sometimes it's so bad I start shaking.

I just want to be normal, so he doesn't have to worry
about making me scared.

I just wish I could be what he deserves.

He says he loves me and he would do anything to see me safe and
happy, but I know he feels like it's his fault sometimes.

I want him to be a part of my future, but I feel like he might leave me
because of all this.

I don't know how to not flinch when he's near. It's been a habit for so
long, but I don't want to lose him because of my past.

Female. North Carolina.

He seemed perfect.

He was the guy who would open the car door for you, take you on picnics, and long walks through the park.

He would put down his jacket so you wouldn't walk through a puddle, stare at you and tell you how beautiful you are.

It was not until our last date that I realized this "perfect" guy was not so perfect after all.

He raped me.

It's been more than a year now and the memory still haunts me.

Female. Texas.

I dated this guy for about eight months. Our love was unconditional.

This year, he died in a car accident. I was so terribly crushed, but now I feel his presence, and I know he still loves me.

Even if your partner is gone, that love can still exist.

That's what keeps me going. I still love him to this day, and I always will.

Female. Kentucky.

I have been dating my boyfriend for almost seven months
and we have plans for a future together.

My ex keeps popping up. This ex raped me, got me pregnant, and beat
me till the baby in my stomach died.

I don't want to tell my boyfriend how scared I am, because I don't want
him to be concerned with this situation.

I feel like it's wrong though for me not to be completely open about my
fears to the love of my life.

Female. Texas.

My ex told me he still loved me.

I told him that I wasn't going to go through that again.

All the yelling and fighting, telling me I'm not good enough for him.

For the next two weeks he kept trying to kill himself.

A month later he blamed me for all the mishaps in his life: depression, cutting, drugs, and suicide attempts.

I now wonder every day if he is still alive.

Female. Montana.

i wish

I wish you knew how much I regret what I did and how sorry I am.
If I could go back and start over, I would.

Female. California.

I **wish** you knew that I both
hated and loved you.

Female. Malaysia.

I wish you knew how worthless
and broken you made me feel.

Male. Texas.

I **wish** you knew that all I needed was more time—more time to
apologize, more time to sort things out.
I'm sorry.

Male. UK.

I wish she knew that sometimes I still listen to our playlist.
I don't hear it with that same feeling of love, but it gives me comfort,
and makes me remember how beautiful our story was.

Male. Portugal.

I wish you knew that he treats me better than you did,
and I loved him the whole time.
I am going to marry him, I was never going to marry you.

Female. New York.

I wish I had never cheated on you.
I wish I never broke up with you.
I wish I never had to let go of your hands.
I wish I never lost your love.

Female. Tunisia.

I wish my ex knew that while I was cracking jokes with him and trying to help him through his depression, I was struggling with a severe anxiety disorder.

Female. India.

I wish it hadn't been all my fault.
I just couldn't stop lying to you.
I lost my soulmate.

Male. UK.

I wish you knew how much I miss your smile.
Even after all this time I am still not able to move on.
I guess I will always love you.

Male. India.

I wish I had known how mentally abusive and
verbally disgusting you would be to me.

Female. New York.

I wish you knew how sorry I am for not trying harder.
I loved you so completely and it was stupid of me to end it.

Female. Israel.

                              I wish you knew that since we broke up,
                         I have been trying to find someone else to date.
                         I can't love anyone else as much as I love you.
                              You are the loss that I can't replace.

                                                    Female. Indonesia.

I wish my ex knew that I found out he took the necklace my great-grandfather
gave me and gave it to another girl, telling her it belonged to his mother.

Female. Australia.

I wish you knew that I still miss your voice, laugh, and beautiful smile that
brought me through the hardest of times.
I hate myself every day for the mistakes I made.
I never meant to take advantage of your feelings and not be around
when you needed me most.
I'm so sorry.

Male. Singapore.

I **wish** you knew I'm not sorry I cheated and broke your heart.
You hurt me mentally and sometimes physically.
I don't regret cheating on you multiple times,
or marrying one of your best friends.
You deserved it after everything you put me through.

Female. Florida.

I wish I had told you the truth.
I broke up with you because I'm scared of coming out of the closet for you.

Female. Indiana.

I wish my ex knew I still love him
even though we broke up seven months ago.
It still makes me smile to think of his laugh.
We're not friends anymore, but I wish every day that we were.

Female. California.

He led me on for five long months.
I wish he knew I thought he was the one.
All he said was I deserved better. What kind of explanation is that?

Female. Kansas.

I wish you knew that I never meant to hurt you.

Female. West Virginia.

I wish you knew how hard it broke me when I had to separate our family when you wouldn't get help.

Female. Canada.

I wish you knew that I knew you were going to date the girl you told me not to worry about.

Female. North Carolina.

I wish you knew that I'm sorry I never loved you.

Female. Massachusetts.

I wish she knew how many times she saved me from going into a hypoglycemic coma. Now I am alone, just me and my type 1 diabetes.

Male. Illinois.

I wish you knew how much it hurt when my little brother asked where you went, and I had to tell him you're a cheater who only liked me because of my looks.

Female. Canada.

My girlfriend of six years dumped me because I took her for granted.
I wasn't around when I needed to be.
I just wish she knew I would do anything to get her back.

Male. Ohio.

> **I wish** you knew you are
> the only reason I am still alive.
>
> *Male. Georgia.*

I wish you knew how much pain you put me through, so you don't do it again, and one day you can treat another girl right.

Female. UK.

> **I wish** my ex knew that I still love her.
> I never meant to break up with her, I just needed space.
>
> *Male. Texas.*

I wish you knew that I have loved you for the last ten years and have never stopped.
I pray that you come back to me and stay this time.

Female. Poland.

I wish you knew that I am fully aware of how long
you were cheating on me.
You didn't get away with it.

Female. Indiana.

I want to try again but slowly and without other people getting involved,
because you bring out the best in me.

Female. Texas.

I wish you knew that on the night you broke up with me,
I was going to tell you I love you.

Female. Ohio.

I wish you knew how often I still wonder
if you overcame your anxiety and depression.

Female. Bulgaria.

I wish you knew I have never deleted our message history.

Female. Indonesia.

I wish my ex knew that I'm so proud of him.
He realized he didn't want to date me, or any other females for that matter.
He took a shot and went on a date with a really great guy.
I'm so glad he's still a part of my life.

Female. Ohio.

I wish you knew that you were enough for me,
and that I would love you forever if only you would let me.

I don't miss you.
I don't love you.

I just long for the happy ending that we were going to have.
You were not a game, you were the end game.

Female. UK.

to my ex

To my ex,

You didn't deserve what I did to you.

I gave up on you.

I should've carried us both, but I was selfish and saved myself only.

You deserve someone who loves you with all their heart, but that somebody isn't me.

Thank you for making me a better person, loving me, being my backbone, my secret keeper, and my best friend.

I hope one day you forgive me, and find someone who treats you the way you deserve to be treated.

Female. Egypt.

To my ex,

You destroyed my life, cheated on me, and abandoned me while I raised our children and battled cancer.

You returned to make my life hell, break my bones, and my spirit.

I took our babies and ran. I survived!

You didn't break me.

I met someone else who showed me real love.

Keep your poison and get over me.

You were right, I am an amazing woman, and you didn't deserve me!

Female. Canada.

To my ex,

My skin still smells like you.

I still can feel the spot where you last touched me. Breathing hurts.

And I'm choking on my tears.

I can't believe you're gone. I can't believe it's real.

In my dreams I begged you to come back.
I begged you to love me again.

But as soon as I woke up I realized that you wouldn't be coming back.

The love I gave you wasn't enough to make you stay.

I'd rather die than feel like this any longer.

Female. Switzerland.

To my ex,

You may have hit me, ignored my lack of consent, and tried to ruin my life.

But now whose life is worse?

You're going to prison for what you've done, and I've found real love. My new life has just begun.

You got what you deserved.

You better pray that if there's a God they forgive you, because nobody else will.

Female. UK.

To my ex,

I miss you. I know I messed up. I didn't realize it at the time.

I knew I needed to change, but it was too late when I finally understood.

I'm so sorry I disappointed you, and I know this all needs time. I respect this, but as time goes on, I hope that there is a chance for us.

I'm changing. In a good way.

The change is slow, but I'm changing into a better me.

I realize there is so much good to feel once you change from a toxic mindset to a positive one.

Male. Ireland.

To my ex,

Your eyes were cold.

Your hands were heat caressing every curve of my ice-cold body.

But it was only cold for you.

Because I didn't want your heat.

Female. Illinois.

To my ex,

I miss you. So damn much.

Why did you have to die?

I miss your voice and arms around me.
You have no idea how much it hurt when you left.

I want you back, you know I do . . . and I hope you want me back too.

Every night I think of joining you, but I stop myself,
because my friends tell me to move on.

Somehow it's not that easy. I want you and only you.

Come back to me please . . . Or I will join you.
Whatever I have do to see you again.

Female. New York.

To my ex,

We were as toxic as they come.

The arguing and jealousy had hit an all-time high, but so had the love and passion.

But then you got into drugs and I walked away.

I'll always love you and I'm so proud of you.

You've gotten your life together and are clean and doing well now.

I know we still talk sometimes to check in with each other.

I miss you, and I miss us, but we can't ever be together again.

Female. New York.

To my ex,

After almost two years with you, I forgot what respect was.

I put so much into our relationship and got nothing in return.

I faked a smile daily as you controlled everything in my life.

Now I'm with a man who words will not do justice for.

I can confidently say he loves me and truly makes me a better person.

I can't remember a time with you where my cheeks hurt from smiling so much.

You deserve to see us happy every day as you watch in silence.

Female. Texas.

To my ex,

I miss you so much, and I wish things were just like before.

I miss the pattern of hearts we'd text each other before going to bed. I miss the love you gave me every day.

One day I hope we realize we were meant for each other.

If not, then the time we had together was still worth every second. I know we were young and dumb but we knew what love was with each other.

We planned our wedding in Hawaii and planned our kids' futures. We planned on living in New York together, then moving to California to start our family.

I miss keeping my ringer on at night waiting for you to call me because you needed me or missed me. I miss waking up to "I love you" texts.

That's all gone now, and with you gone, a part of my heart left with you. I need that love back and I need you back.

Every night I hope you call me to say "I love you and I miss you."

Male. New York.

To my ex,

I used to care about you and love you, until I realized how pathetic I was to be crying over someone who simply didn't care.

You hurt me, made me feel worthless, stupid, and unimportant.

I let you control me, but I'm moving on.

You did, however, teach me one important lesson: Never stay with someone who clearly doesn't want to be with you.

Male. UK.

To my ex,

If you start to miss me.

Remember.

I didn't walk away.

You let me go.

Male. UK.

To my ex,

You changed me in the best and worst ways. You picked me up just to push me down. Used me and hurt me more than once.

At one point I thought you were the one. You were the only person I opened my heart fully to during my darkest time.

But you taught me in the multiple times you left and came back, that I should be much more than the sex and comfort you used me for.

Now I'm getting married, and I still expect you to pop up again right before I say "I do."

I'll always love you, but I hate you, and I truly hope one day you fall down as I hard as I did.

I hope someone lets you down harder than the times you let me down. Thank you for showing me what I was truly lacking in my life.

You wouldn't have been a good mother anyway.

Male. Illinois.

To my ex,

We were beautiful together. We spent every day
together doing what we both loved.

When your father committed suicide, you took on a huge
role to keep your family strong. It was hard to deal with,
and I tried my best to be your rock.

You said I was your only happiness.

I was also your first phone call when you needed your
emotions to be let out. I was the first person you cried to.

But time passed and your strength was diminishing. You said
you needed a friend more than a girlfriend, and I became insecure.

You didn't want us to change, but I couldn't handle just being a friend.

The day before I left to go to Europe for two months,
you said you would miss me more than anything.

That was hard to believe once I returned and found
out you'd cheated and had a new girlfriend.

I feel that no matter how far we let things get away from us,
we always come back to each other.

But I don't know.

Female. Texas.

To my ex,

You taught me a number of things.

1. Don't believe everything you hear.
2. Don't fall in love with losers like you.
3. I need to be the baddest bitch I can be.
4. You don't matter to me anymore.

Female. Canada.

To my ex,

You suffocated me so much, that when we stopped talking, I could breathe for the first time.

You pulled me away from the people that truly made me the happiest.

You made me forget family is forever.

You victimized yourself as a method of keeping me.

After you, I was able to find real love, love that doesn't hurt.

Female. Arizona.

To my ex,

I love you more than anything in the world.

You were taken away by angels as you lost your battle to cancer.

I refuse to let go of you.

You were and still are my world.

I will never meet someone like you ever again. I miss you so much and I love you.

Female. New Zealand.

To my ex,

We were really close before we started dating, so I thought I knew you. You were kind, caring, loving, and an all-around amazing person.

But as we got closer, you changed. Your sweet words turned into knives, and I started believing things I shouldn't have.

I started to change for you, to make you happy, and to make sure you stayed in love with me.

I started to hate my body because you made me believe it was worthless.

I started to become distant with my family because you told me I didn't need them; I only needed you.

When I finally left, you told me everything you did with other girls while we were together.

I wanted to run, but I couldn't.

It was like a train wreck—I wanted to look away but with every word, I finally realized you weren't worth my tears and sadness.

While I am nowhere close to being perfect, I am finally happy with how I look, and I am finally back to how I was with my family, and I'm happy with who I am.

I don't need you anymore. I'm free.

Female. Ohio.

To my ex,

Thank you.

Thank you for treating me so poorly, because I now know that I can never allow myself to go through that again.

Thank you.

Thank you for making me understand that I deserve so much better.

Thank you.

Thank you for being so awful, so I could find someone who cares for me.

I truly hope whoever you're with next you treat like a queen.

Nobody deserves to ever go through what you put me through. I wouldn't wish that on my worst enemy.

I'm with someone now who truly cares about me for who I am, regardless of all the flaws.

Someone who's not embarrassed of me for being a little crazy and outgoing.

Thank you from the bottom of my heart.

Despite all the cruel things you've done and said to me, I truly wish only happiness for you.

Female. North Carolina.

To my ex,

You promised not to let me go, but that's exactly what you did.

You ended it when I was at my most vulnerable.

You shattered me and I tried my best over and over again to keep you, but you had moved on.

Fast forward two years, you came back asking to "meet up," as if I was stupid enough to do that.

You begged to see me, trying to apologize because you realized a little too late you hurt me.

Do you have any idea how many sleepless nights I spent crying, knowing that you were with someone else?

Do you have any idea how many times I wrote my feelings about you on a piece of paper and flushed it down the toilet?

Now that you're back, I'm gone, darling.

No, not because I'm seeking revenge, but because I know I deserve far better than someone who destroyed me.

You never loved me, you loved the attention I gave you.

Female. Canada.

To my ex,

Now that everything is over I know I made the best decision of my life.

We have two kids, and I couldn't justify living with a cheater my entire life.

I gave you way too many chances, and you decided to ruin every single one of them.

It's been almost four years.

I'm happy I found someone who loves me unconditionally, and you should know he's a great stepfather to your kids.

Female. Illinois.

To my ex,

You've realized how truly amazing you are.

You are stunning and smart, graceful and funny.

I love you with all my heart, I don't think I will ever stop loving you.

When we broke up, we stayed friends.

Now I see you every day.

I tell you my deepest secrets.

You are the only person that I actually trust, but I can't tell you how much I love you. That would make everything too complicated.

You make the world a better place.

When you walk into a room, the whole demeanor changes, everyone lights up and everything seems happier. Keep being you.

I know that you will probably never love me the way that I love you.

Maybe one day I will have the courage to say this to you in person. I love you.

Female. Colorado.

To my ex,

I wonder how long it's going to take for me to realize I don't need you.

How many days am I going to lay in bed with tears running down my face?

What if all of this had never happened? What if we'd never met, and our memories never existed?

I want to remember you as that person who made me laugh, made me smile.

The person who gave me chills down the side of my body every time I heard your voice.

The person who was there for me, even during my worst times.

But that person, the person I had fallen in love with, is gone.

Right after you left, all my hopes and dreams disappeared right before my eyes.

The rest of my future torn apart.

I gave you my heart, and you took it away.

There will forever be a dark place, with the memories of the fights and scars.

And after all of this I never even got a "sorry."

Female. Wisconsin.

healing

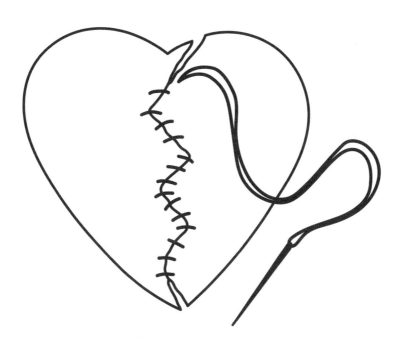

Heartbreak sucks,
but rising from the ashes is amazing.

Female. Canada.

To the next person I date,

It will take a long time for me to open up to you.

I have been broken, crushed, and stomped on many times.

At times I will be difficult or quiet. At times I will not believe you, and I will be frustrating.

No matter how much love you show, it will be hard for me to believe it's real because I have been taught that people hurt and break you.

I have it stuck in my head that nobody loves me and nobody ever will. That it's all just some sick joke.

Stay with me.

Stay with me and the insecurities will go away.
And I will finally open up.
And when I do, it will be worth the wait.

Male. California.

You loved me.
You promised.
You broke that promise.

But I got up.
I am strong.
I will love again.

Female. Michigan.

To the next person I date,

You need to know I am broken, but that I am capable of loving you with every broken piece.

I won't be unfaithful, and I won't just give up on you.

There is one catch—my son will always come first.

You have to love and accept him even more so than you do me.

He is an amazing boy, and has the biggest heart.

If you can accept me and love him, we will do just fine.

Female. Arizona.

It has been almost a year since my ex left
and broke not just my heart, but my whole being.

I started working on me. Finding different hobbies. I discovered art.

A couple of weeks ago, a guy I'd been hanging out with
for months told me he liked me.

I realized I had started to like him too, but I was scared.

Now we are exclusive but taking it slow.

I never thought my heart could be happy again.

Never thought I would get butterflies and be that kind of excited again.

While it's not the same, it's a really good kind of different.

Female. Kansas.

To the next person I date,

Believe in me.

I ask that you support me in what I am trying to accomplish in my life.

I have big expectations for myself, and I don't need another guy telling me what I can't do.

Trust me.

Don't try and close me off from the world because you worry someone else is going to take me from you.

That's all I ask for.

Female. Wisconsin.

To myself,

He may have broken you.
He may have played you like a fool.
He may have made you believe he actually cared.

But it's okay.

You're beautiful.
You're amazing, and you WILL find someone else that actually cares.

Female. Georgia.

To the next person I date,

Time.
Effort.
Consistency.

I don't care how much money you have.
I don't need expensive gifts.

I fell in love with you, not your wallet.

Female. South Africa.

I was able to heal by finding someone who doesn't just walk through my light and dance with my angels, but someone who can also love my darkness and silence my demons.

Female. Tennessee.

To my future boyfriend or girlfriend,

I have anxiety, and I'm going to get really jealous of anyone who is close to you.

This doesn't mean I don't trust you, because I do with all my heart.

I already know I'll love you with all of my being, and I'll trust you more than anyone else.

But I get protective and jealous because I think that I don't deserve you.

I'll get jealous because I'll think you'll find someone you like better than me.

It's just the anxiety. I love you and trust you, so please just be patient with me.

Female. Pennsylvania.

Let it hurt.
Feel the pain.
Mourn the loss, and the good times you had.

But after that . . .

Pick yourself up and show them what they're missing out on.

Female. Texas.

To myself,

You didn't feel right with him, and that doesn't make you a bad person.

You listened to yourself.

You may not be with anyone right now, and that's okay.

Someday you'll find the right person, and you'll know it's the right person.

You have your best friends, and that's enough love for now.

Don't you dare give up.

Female. Colorado.

To the next person I date,

Loving you will be a challenge for me, because the one before you really messed me up.

I know how deep my love can be, but I gave it to someone who didn't care. I regret that I wasn't enough.

You have to earn my trust.

I'm sorry, but I notice too much, I think too much.

But trust me, the love I'll be giving you, it's going to be like nothing else.

You're always going to be my number one.

There won't be a single moment in which I'm not going to be thinking of you.

Just be loyal, root for me, and you'll never have a shortage of love.

Male. Bangladesh.

To myself,

After years of getting your heart broken, and going through one abusive relationship after another, you have finally found someone who makes you happy.

You never thought you were worthy of being loved and cared for until you met him.

He made you realize you are so much more incredible than you ever realized.

He brought out the happiness in you and made your heart whole.

You did it.

You finally found someone who will always love you. I am so proud of you.

Female. Texas.

My world fell apart at the thought of you leaving.

We've been together for six months now and I've never been so attached to someone.

Your touch makes me feel like my heart will explode.

When I first met you, I felt so alone.

You fixed me and repaired what was broken.

You made my heart complete again and showed me that love doesn't have to have violent episodes.

Female. Tennessee.

To the next person I date,

I have scars on my arms. What happened to me last year destroyed me.

But now I'm fine. I'm ready for a new relationship!

I'm ready for you.

I'm strong now, and I can handle new things.

Hope to meet you soon.

Female. Germany.

At first it was hard to even breathe.

I felt like I was locked in a cage, and my soul was burning.

It was unbearable. I just wanted to run until I was numb to all my feelings.

Time heals, though. One day I woke up and found peace.

It was the most liberating feeling I have ever had. I knew I had survived.

Breakups never get easy, but it's nice to know our hearts have the ability to heal.

Female. Romania.

To myself,

You're not weak.
You're amazing.
He didn't deserve you.

He broke your heart, when you sacrificed everything for him.

You can do it, you can get over him. You're capable of doing anything.

It's time you start appreciating yourself more.

Whoever doesn't want you, it's their loss.

Female. Egypt.

To the next person I date,

I have experienced all sorts of love now.

Because of this, I know what I am looking for, and I know what it feels like.

The last guy I dated showed me love in a beautiful way. I wish our circumstances were different and we could have stayed together. But it didn't work out that way.

I am excited to meet you, the next guy, because I know that I will be ready, healthier, and able to live life to the fullest.

Female. California.

Your weakness was believing that your ex
was the key to your happiness.

Now you can move on, be free, and start to breathe again.

Healing can begin.

Female. Lebanon.

To myself,

You're happy, finally.

You found someone who you mean the world to, and you were finally able to open up to him.

You were able to overcome everything you hated about yourself.

In fact, you love everything about yourself.

You love that you are so strange, and you are unapologetically yourself.

You don't fake it anymore. And you are fine with that.
You are SO happy now.

Female. Ohio.

author's note

The stories in this book are ones that often go untold but need to be heard.

I'd like to thank all of the contributors who have bravely come forward.

Telling our stories, especially the hurtful ones, allows the conversation and healing to begin.

My Date My Story and other projects I am working on can be seen at KoreVoices.com